MANAGING YOUR BOSS

MANAGING YOUR BOSS

**Patti Hathaway and
Susan D Schubert**

KOGAN
PAGE

First published in the United States of America enti-
tled *Managing Upward* in 1992 by Crisp Publications
Inc, 1200 Hamilton Court, Menlo Park, CA 94025,
USA.

This edition first published in Great Britain in 1993
by Kogan Page Ltd, 120 Pentonville Road, London
N1 9JN.

British Library Cataloguing in Publication Data

A CIP record for this book is available from the British Library.

ISBN 0-7494-1078-7

Typeset by BookEns Ltd, Baldock, Herts.
Printed and bound in Great Britain by Clays Ltd, St Ives plc.

Contents

Preface   **7**

1. **Introduction**   **9**
   What is a boss? 9; Why are you reading this
   book? 11; Defining the partnership and how it can
   work better 11; Think about your situation 13;
   Clarify your relationship 14

2. **Focusing on the Big Picture**   **15**
   Where do I start? 15; Other ways to find out your
   boss's priorities 23; Blend goals 24; Blocks to goal
   achievement 24; Overcoming blocks 25

3. **Communicate with Impact**   **28**
   What is effective communication? 28;
   Communication gaps 32; How well do you
   comprehend or listen? 34

4. **Talk's Not Cheap: Building Bridges via Meetings**   **38**
   Let's talk! 39; Before you jump in 39; Getting
   started 40; The high cost of meetings 42; If your
   boss is the meeting leader 44

5. **Confronting with Compassion**   **47**
   How can you criticise your manager? 47; Five Ss of
   providing unsolicited feedback 50

6. **How to Read Your Boss**   54
    Reading your boss 55

7. **The Care and Feeding of a Boss**   62
    Six ways to become a star 62; Successful employee
    actions 64; Praising upwards 66; Things bosses don't
    want 67

8. **Managing Time-Management Monsters**   70
    Productivity principles 70; Interruptions 72;
    Changing priorities 74; Coping with multiple
    bosses 74; Lack of information 76; Unavailable
    boss 76; Disorganised boss 77

9. **Coping with Dreadful Bosses**   78
    All bosses are not created equal 78; Intolerable boss
    behaviour 79; What can you do? 80; Risk to action
    steps diagram 81; Good guy/bad guy 85; The
    bottleneck boss 88

10. **Snakes or Ladders**   91
    Assess yourself 91; Evaluating your score
    sheet 94; How to achieve good performance
    evaluations 96; Handling criticism 98

11. **The Final Episode**   105

Further Reading from Kogan Page   107

Preface

As professional speakers and trainers, we are constantly asked for suggestions on how to manage more effectively. Regardless of geographical region, industry or profession, people want to know how they can be more productive and enhance their careers, in spite of, or with the help of, their bosses.

The ideas and strategies presented in this book come from the people who have attended our seminars and the organisations which we have consulted. We have tested the concepts and exercises with employees who tried them. Compiled in this book are ideas that work.

Our challenge to you is not only to read the book, but also to experience the strategies. Best wishes to you as you begin the challenge of managing your career by managing your boss!

Patti Hathaway
Susan Schubert

CHAPTER 1
Introduction

This book is for everyone with a boss. It is written for everyone who works for someone else, including first-line supervisors, mid-level managers, secretaries and team leaders. The basic concepts are applicable in manufacturing, education, profit-driven and nonprofit organisations where teamwork between employees and their managers can benefit individuals, the total organisation and, ultimately, its customers.

What is a boss?

Several words are used interchangeably to designate a person who receives direction, training, correction, etc, from another. These words include employee, direct report, staff.

The words boss, manager and supervisor mean those responsible by title and actions for leading, training and evaluating other people. Usually these people have a designated management position in the organisation. However, they may assume supervisory roles in time-limited situations such as task forces, committees or when an employee 'fills in' for a supervisor.

Who manages whom?

Employees share the responsibility for managing the relationship between themselves and their superiors. Exercised with skill and initiative rather than passivity and powerlessness, that role can strengthen everyone's motivation and productivity.

Authors John J Gabarro and John P Kotter state that 'managing upwards' is the art of *consciously* improving collaboration with one's boss, to gain the best personal and organisational outcomes. It is not just superficial manipulating and empty praise. Alice Kelvin writes that many subordinates avoid upward managing because of earlier experiences with authority figures. The role of employee seems like the passive early role of a child or student who unquestioningly accepts instruction from superiors – parents and teachers. By breaking the pattern of passivity, employees can become truly motivated, based on feelings of competence, self-control and perceived results.

What this book will do

This book will help you to improve your working arrangement with your boss, if you use the strategies outlined. Your positive actions will help you to:

- Clarify misunderstandings that obstruct the quality and quantity of your work
- Manage yourself better so you can be a role model for your boss and colleagues
- Take calculated risks
- Turn anger and frustration into constructive assertiveness
- Decide when the relationship is not manageable.

Benefits

Rarely, if ever, are employees trained in techniques necessary for creating more effective collaboration with their supervisors. A solid professional relationship improves employees' job performances and their mental and physical health. If you master upward management techniques, you can achieve a number of personal and professional goals for yourself.

To obtain maximum results from this book, complete the exercises. Some you can do alone; others you must do with your supervisor. The exercises start with general, fairly easy questions and topics. They build on acquired skills, as you continue through the book, and end with complex situations based on actual circumstances.

Why are you reading this book?

Following is a list of potential outcomes from using the techniques in this book. Please tick those benefits that you would like to experience.

Exercise 1. Benefits

_____ 1. Reduce physical and mental stress
_____ 2. Increase opportunity for recognition and promotion
_____ 3. Implement ideas
_____ 4. Increase self-confidence, motivation and morale
_____ 5. Increase respect from colleagues
_____ 6. Help to make a career decision about whether to leave job
_____ 7. Anticipate and avoid problems with my boss
_____ 8. Improve the quality and quantity of my work
_____ 9. Increase enjoyment of my job
_____ 10. Other (specify)_____ .

Concentrate on your desired benefits as you take these important steps towards strengthening cooperative collaboration between yourself and your supervisor.

Defining the partnership and how it can work better

A satisfying relationship between a manager and employees may be compared to a successful partnership. People enter a partnership because they perceive that by combining their efforts and resources they can achieve their goals better than if they work solo. The manager and employee may have written documents such as a contract, job description, policies and procedures that specify their contributions – what each gives; and compensation – what each gets. However, a great part of working relationships is based on historical practices and unwritten assumptions. To improve the working partnership, vague assumptions must be converted into specific agreements. Typical examples of the contribution/compensation partnership follow.

Contribution/Compensation partnership

The Employer gives	The Employee gives
Security	Time
Appreciation	Knowledge
Training	Skills
Advice	Dependability
Money	
Tools and equipment to produce work	
The Employer gets	**The Employee gets**
Quality work	Money
Loyalty	Appreciation
Commitment	Challenge
Dependability	
Recognition	

Think about your situation

Now think about your own working partnership. List two or three essential elements in your relationship with your boss. See if you can determine what your boss gets from you and gives to you. Then, complete both sides of the following equation.

Exercise 2. Compensation/Contribution partnership

My boss gives me
(Example: opportunities for additional education.)

I give my boss
(Example: specialised skills in solving engineering problems.)

_____   _____

_____   _____

_____   _____
_____   _____
_____   _____
_____   _____
_____   _____
_____   _____

My boss receives
(Example: work that is
thorough and usually
completed on time.)

I receive
(Example: challenging work.)

_____   _____
_____   _____
_____   _____
_____   _____
_____   _____
_____   _____
_____   _____

Exercise 3. Level of understanding between you and your supervisor

By completing these lists, you have begun to get a better understanding of your relationship with your boss. Now review your answers by responding to the following questions with 'Yes', 'No', or 'Unsure'.

_____ **1.** Do you understand what your manager wants you to contribute to your relationship?

_____ **2.** Do you receive equitable compensation – salary plus intangible appreciation, etc – for the effort, knowledge, skills and abilities you contribute to the organisation?

_____ 3. Does your supervisor know what you need from him or her to perform your work satisfactorily?

_____ 4. Do you think your boss believes he or she is receiving a fair exchange – commitment, results, etc – from you?

_____ 5. Do you and your supervisor collectively agree that your partnership is beneficial for each of you?

Even if you answered 'Yes' to all of these questions, you can improve your work situation in many practical ways by applying upward management skills.

Clarify your relationship

To obtain more clarification, you may wish to do one or more of the following:

- Review your latest performance evaluation to decide where you need to improve and see what your manager emphasises
- Review job description, work plans, goals and objectives
- Talk to associates who may have ideas about how to improve communication with your mutual supervisor
- Hold a meeting with your boss.

Once you have a better idea of the relationship you would like to have with your boss, it is time to look at what this relationship can do for both you and your organisation.

CHAPTER 2

Focusing on the Big Picture

When organisations lack clear focus, they are less successful than they could be because they lack direction and purpose. Employees who lack clarity of focus and purpose find it difficult to achieve career success. An important key to an effective partnership between employees and managers is establishing team goals, priorities and plans to achieve those goals.

Where do I start?

Most organisations hire employees to fit a job description and then tell them why they are there and what they should do. Employees function quite easily without their own personal goals and direction. However, personal goals can provide you with energy, enthusiasm and a clear plan of how to get things done in your job. Unless you clarify how your personal goals are connected to organisational direction, you may become frustrated or burned out.

Blessing/White, a US personal and corporate growth training company developed a career development programme called Managing Personal Growth (MPG). MPG employs a model – modified here – to explain how an organisation's goals and values intersect with an individual's goals and values to increase productivity and effectiveness.

The intersection in the middle of the model represents your job. If your organisation or your boss is very clear about the company's goals and values, that will translate into clear expectations for you. The result is that the company will probably get what it wants from you: maximum productivity. But if the organisation and manager are unfocused about their expectations and priorities, employees will be unclear about what to do and productivity will decline. Clear organisational goals and values provide employees with a sense of direction and mission.

MPG model

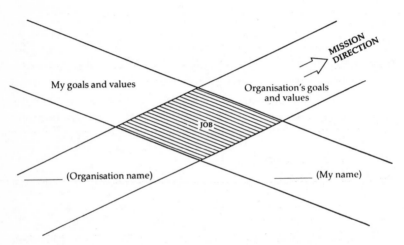

You may be productive because the organisation has defined its goals and expectations for you, yet you may not have defined what would make you happy or satisfied in that job. When you define your values, you gain energy and purpose. See the model on page 17. When you tie these two components together – organisation direction with personal energy – you will be much closer to maximum satisfaction and productivity than most employees.

Exercise 1. A goal self-assessment

1. The purpose of my organisation is:

_____

_____

_____

_____

2. The purpose of my job is:

_____

_____

_____

_____

3. Some of the daily responsibilities in my job are:

_____

_____

_____

_____

4. The three most important priorities of my job are:
  1) _____

    _____

    _____

2) _____

_____

3) _____

_____

If you had difficulty completing the information in Exercise 1, you may find that you and your boss are not in tune. To create an effective partnership with your boss, it is essential to know your boss's most important priorities.

Exercise 2. Questionnaire for employees

Please complete this questionnaire on your own. Tick those that apply.

About your manager

1. Does your manager prefer to receive information through:
   - ____ Memos ____ Phone calls
   - ____ Formal meetings ____ Informal meetings
   - ____ Other (specify)_____

2. What is your manager's preferred style of working?
   - ____ Organised and highly structured
   - ____ Moderately organised and structured
   - ____ Little organisation or structure
   - ____ Other (specify)_____

3. What are your manager's top three organisational priorities?
   1. _____
   2. _____
   3. _____

4. What are your manager's top three personal priorities?
   1. _____
   2. _____
   3. _____

5. What is your manager's attitude towards conflict?
    ____ Thrives on it   ____ Tries to minimise it
    ____ Other (specify)_____

6. What are your manager's three outstanding strengths?
    1. _____
    2. _____
    3. _____

7. What is your manager's greatest pressure?_____

8. What will your manager say are your three greatest strengths?
    1. _____
    2. _____
    3. _____

9. What will your manager say are your top three organisational priorities?
    1. _____
    2. _____
    3. _____

10. What will your manager say are your top three personal priorities?
    1. _____
    2. _____
    3. _____

About you – Change perspective to focus on your point of view

11. Do you prefer to receive information through:
    ____ Memos   ____ Phone calls
    ____ Formal meetings   ____ Informal meetings
    ____ Other (specify)_____

12. What is your preferred style of working?
    ____ Organised and highly structured
    ____ Moderately organised and structured
    ____ Little organisation or structure
    ____ Other (specify)_____

13. What is your greatest pressure?_____

14. What is your attitude towards conflict?
    ____ Thrive on it   ____ Try to minimise it
    ____ Other (specify)_____

Exercise 3. Questionnaire for bosses
Please copy this questionnaire and ask your boss to complete it
from the management perspective. Then compare your answers
and come to an understanding about your priorities and working styles.

About you – The boss

1. Do you prefer to receive information through:
    ____ Memos   ____ Phone calls
    ____ Formal meetings   ____ Informal meetings
    ____ Other (specify)_____

2. What is your preferred style of working?
    ____ Organised and highly structured
    ____ Moderately organised and structured
    ____ Little organisation or structure
    ____ Other (specify)_____

3. What are your top three organisational priorities?
    1. _____
    2. _____
    3. _____

4. What are your top three personal priorities?
    1. _____

2. _____
3. _____

5. What is your attitude towards conflict?

   ____ Thrive on it   ____ Try to minimise it
   ____ Other (specify)_____

6. What do you see as your three outstanding strengths?
   1. _____
   2. _____
   3. _____

7. What is your greatest pressure?_____

8. What are your employee's three greatest strengths?
   1. _____
   2. _____
   3. _____

9. What are your employee's top three organisational goals?
   1. _____
   2. _____
   3. _____

10. What are your employee's top three personal priorities?
   1. _____
   2. _____
   3. _____

11. Does your employee prefer to receive information through:

   ____ Memos   ____ Phone calls
   ____ Formal meetings   ____ Informal meetings
   ____ Other (specify)_____

12. What is your employee's preferred style of working?
   ____ Organised and highly structured
   ____ Moderately organised and structured

_____ Little organisation or structure
_____ Other (specify)_____

13. What is your employee's greatest pressure?_____

14. What is your employee's attitude towards conflict?
    _____ Thrives on it   _____ Tries to minimise it
    _____ Other (specify)_____

Exercise 4. Check your assumptions
If you had difficulty with the answers concerning your supervisor, your priorities and organisation's goals, discuss them with your boss. Here are other strategies that may help. Tick the approaches that you want to use.

_____ 1. Ask about goals during a one-to-one meeting with your supervisor. You might say, 'I have been trying to improve my performance and it would be helpful to have a clearer picture of how my work goals fit in with yours and the company's.' (Make a copy of Exercise 3. Give it to your boss if you have not already done so.)

_____ 2. Encourage discussion during a staff meeting. You could say, 'As a member of this working team, I feel it's important for us to agree on common goals. Could we discuss them and write them down?'

_____ 3. Send a written memo: 'To make sure I am going in the right direction, I have developed a list of my five key goals for the next six months. Please review them and let me know if I am on target. Correct any areas of misunderstanding.'

_____ 4. Encourage your boss and associates to share progress reports regarding collective and individual achievement of goals and objectives. Use team meetings to discuss problems and ways to overcome them by working together more effectively.

Add more

_____

_____

_____

_____

_____

_____

_____

_____

_____

_____

Other ways to find out your boss's priorities

Asking questions is not the only way to assess your boss's priorities. Just by being alert, you can pick up valuable information. Be on the lookout for expressions and ideas used most often by your company's management personnel. Here are some ways you can go about collecting these phrases:

- Read messages posted on notice boards, company newsletters, memos from your chief executive, annual reports and stock market reports. Highlight how your company describes its goals, competition and problems. Try to find repeated key words such as 'innovation', 'service to customers', 'excellence', 'commitment'.
- Listen to themes that arise in meetings. For example, one committee includes this goal on every meeting agenda: 'To involve total membership in decision making'.
- In small businesses, goals may not be stated so publicly. Listen to what gets everyone excited and frustrated. You may hear people talking about 'building repeat business' and 'making sure that everything is done right the first time'.

Blend goals

Your goals and your supervisor's goals do not need to be identical, but they need to be compatible. Supervisors and employees can start out with opposing goals and change them to complementary goals.

Incompatible goals

Boss: 'To improve teamwork in my department.'
Employee: 'To work independently on projects I can control totally.'

Compatible goals

Boss: 'To improve teamwork in my department.'
Employee: 'To work collaboratively with my associates on project teams and to target a few projects or parts of team projects that I can handle independently.'

Exercise 5. Compatible goals
Based upon the discussion with my boss, we agreed that my organisational priorities are:

_____

_____

_____

_____

_____

_____

_____

Blocks to goal achievement

Even after you and your supervisor agree on professional

goals, achieving those goals may require the ability to overcome barriers or 'blocks'. A block is anything that prevents you from reaching desired results, causing frustration and pressure. Typical blocks include:

- Personal problems such as poor health, anxiety about family, lack of knowledge or skills and low self-esteem
- Stress caused by the organisational environment, including constant criticism, rumours, poor communication, unclear expectations or directions, poor physical working conditions and inadequate supplies
- External pressures such as economic recession, low customer demand and excessive competition

Blocks to good achievement are illustrated in this diagram:

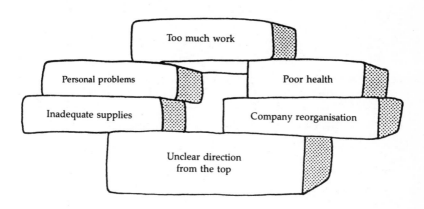

Overcoming blocks

One of the most valuable skills an employee can bring to any workplace is the ability to overcome obstacles while remaining flexible and calm. Over the page is a list of typical blocks to an effective employee–employer partnership, with suggestions for how to become a 'block buster'. Think about how they apply to you.

Blocks	What I could do to overcome blocks
1. There is just too much work	Organise work better. Suggest that our department/team discuss how we can work more cooperatively and reduce unnecessary interruptions. Document work load and suggest taking on permanent or temporary staff.
2. Poor health	Exercise regularly. Eat breakfast every day. Have a check-up. Have specialists study workplace hazards, such as ventilation, lighting, workstation ergonomics, and make recommendations.
3. Boss has family/ personal problems	Be sympathetic but avoid in-depth personal discussions.
4. Supplies are inadequate	Serve on a problem-solving team to investigate alternatives.
5. The company is reorganising	Stay calm and flexible. Avoid spreading rumours. Find out the facts.
6. Directions from the top are unclear	Ask questions, write memos, offer feedback.
7. The economy is in recession	Suggest ways to reduce costs and waste.

Exercise 6. Create an action plan

Now list your own ideas for becoming a block buster.

Blocks	What I could do to overcome blocks
1.	
2.	
3.	

CHAPTER 3
Communicate with Impact

The quality of a partnership between an employee and a boss depends on the quality of communication between the two. Communication does not imply that supervisors and staff will agree with each other, but at its best, communication means they will understand each other.

What is effective communication?

Sometimes our own feelings of powerlessness or inferiority may prevent us from communicating effectively with a boss. These feelings of inferiority can come from past professional experiences, our own parent–child relationship, or the negative things we say to ourselves. ('My boss knows a lot more about this than I do – I'm sure my view isn't needed.') Although you need to have a healthy respect for your manager, it is also important to view your own talents and contributions as worthwhile and important.

If you recognise that it is difficult to talk to your supervisor, plan ways to counteract those negative emotions. It is particularly important with new bosses to come to the relationship without preconceived notions about what they may be or should be like.

Before meetings with your manager, practise saying positive things to yourself or a colleague, such as, 'I have a lot of experience with this organisation and my analytical skills are excellent. I know you will want my input on project xyz . . .' Write an outline of what you want to cover. The more you can plan the conversation, the more effective your interaction with your boss will be.

The two primary ingredients of effective communication are effective expression and effective comprehension. When both these ingredients are present, you can achieve understanding between people.

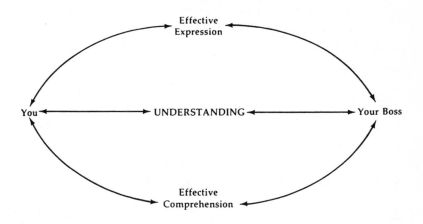

When effective expression or effective comprehension are not present, instead of *understanding* you will experience a *communication gap*.

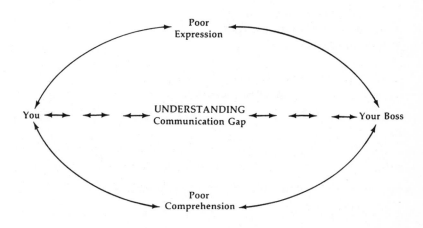

> 'The spoken word belongs half to him who speaks,
> and half to him who hears.'
>
> French proverb

Exercise 1. How well do you express yourself?

How you express yourself has an incredible impact on your professional relationships. The examples below will help you to assess how successful you are in achieving effective communication. Read each of the following statements and tick the appropriate column.

Examples	Very descriptive of me	Somewhat descriptive of me	Not descriptive of me
1. In conversations with my boss, my words generally do not come out the way I want them to.			
2. When I am trying to explain something, others have a tendency to put words in my mouth.			
3. I usually assume my boss knows what I am trying to say without my explaining it.			
4. It is difficult to express my ideas if they are different from my boss's ideas.			
5. In conversations with my boss, I do not try to be empathetic.			
6. I generally talk more than my supervisor.			

Examples	Very descriptive of me	Somewhat descriptive of me	Not descriptive of me
7. I find it difficult to express myself to my boss when I am angry.	_____	_____	_____
8. I am unaware of how my tone of voice affects others.	_____	_____	_____
9. I sometimes say things that hurt others or create conflict.	_____	_____	_____
10. I do not disagree with my boss because I am afraid he/she will get angry.	_____	_____	_____
11. I find it uncomfortable to compliment others.	_____	_____	_____
12. When a problem arises between me and my manager, I cannot discuss it without becoming angry.	_____	_____	_____
13. I do not try to use words that my manager will understand.	_____	_____	_____
14. I ramble when I try to explain something.	_____	_____	_____

Discussion

Review the answers in the 'Very descriptive of me' column. These are the areas that probably hinder your manager's comprehension of what you say. Think about your relationship with your boss. Jot down the communication areas in which you need to improve and examples of how those problem areas have affected your relationship to date.

1. Problem area: _____

   Result: _____

2. Problem area: _____

   Result: _____

3. Problem area: _____

   Result: _____

Communication gaps

Before you can devise strategies for improving the way you express yourself, you need to understand the causes of ineffective communication. Some of the gaps in your communication may occur for the following reasons:

1. **Vocabulary failure.** Words are tools for thought and expression. If you do not know the exact meaning of words, you cannot think with precision; therefore, your ability to express ideas and feelings is also diminished. Studies indicate that people with the largest vocabularies are also highest in position and pay.

   Action ideas. Read everything you can get your hands on.

2. **Talking too much.** Some of us judge others' acceptance of us by how much we talk and how much others listen to us. But you can overwhelm your listeners with conversation until they become confused, bored or both.

   Action ideas. Learn to be word-effective. Do not waste words or ramble. Get to the point, keep to the point. Become aware of how much you dominate conversations and why. Do you begin talking more when you are nervous or uncomfortable? Try to pick up on your listener's interest level.

3. **Speaking before thinking.** Sometimes we speak before thinking. You may not think through why you want to speak; you may not be taking time to assess the best way to express your ideas.

   Action ideas. Stop before you jump into a conversation and ask yourself: What do I want to say? Why do I want to say this? What is the best way for me to get the message across? In a formal setting, you may want to outline your ideas before expressing yourself. For very difficult conversations, it is helpful to practise your comments in advance.

4. **Not testing for understanding.** The speaker may fail to make sure that the listener understands what has been communicated. Testing for understanding minimises the possibility of a communication gap and avoids misunderstandings.

   Action ideas. Ask questions to see if your listener has understood your message. Women generally ask more questions in a conversation than men. They do this several ways, such as ending a statement on a higher pitch, or using tag-ons such as 'OK?', 'All right?' or 'Do you agree?'

Exercise 2. My communication gaps
Listed below are some of the communication gaps that cause problems in the way I express myself:

1. Gap: _____

   Action idea: _____

2. Gap: _____

   Action idea: _____

3. Gap: _____

   Action idea: _____

How well do you comprehend or listen?

Since communication is a two-way process, it is as important to analyse how well you comprehend or listen to others as it is to know how well you express yourself. We spend more than half our day listening, yet we retain very little of what we hear. One study concluded that we hear half of what is said, listen to half of what we hear, understand half of that, believe half of that, and remember only half of that. Translated into an eight-hour day, it means:

> We spend about four hours listening.
> We hear about two hours' worth.
> We listen to one hour's worth.
> We understand 30 minutes of that hour.
> We believe only 15 minutes' worth.
> We remember just under eight minutes' worth.

Exercise 3. Self-assessment in listening

Assess your comprehension and listening skills by evaluating how often you engage in these poor listening habits when listening to your boss:

	Almost always			Almost	never
Problem area	1	2	3	4	5
1. Uninterested in subject matter because it does not affect my job	1	2	3	4	5
2. Over-critical when manager speaks	1	2	3	4	5
3. Interrupt	1	2	3	4	5
4. Focus on details and miss main points	1	2	3	4	5
5. Fake attention because it is 'the same old story'.	1	2	3	4	5
6. Avoid difficult topics	1	2	3	4	5
7. Allow distractions to interfere	1	2	3	4	5
8. Daydream in staff meetings	1	2	3	4	5

9. Allow emotional reactions to certain words or my boss to block the message	1	2	3	4	5
10. Give negative non-verbal cues	1	2	3	4	5

TOTAL_____(out of a possible 50)

Scoring: 50–35:   You are an excellent listener!
                34–29:   You are doing a good job.
                28–23:   You could use some improvement.
       Below 23:   Keep reading!

Capitalise on thought speed

Most people speak at a rate of 125 words per minute, yet can listen at about 500 words per minute. Because of this, you might find that you sometimes daydream, interrupt your boss or fake attention. What you do with your 'extra' thinking time can spell the difference between being an effective or poor listener.

Judge content, not delivery

Many listeners focus only a speaker's appearance or personality. Force yourself to concentrate on the message being communicated and how the information can help you.

Resist distractions

A good listener fights distractions. Sometimes distractions can be easily handled by closing a door, turning off the radio or asking your supervisor to talk more loudly. If you cannot eliminate the distraction, you may simply need to concentrate more. Take notes; this sends the message that your supervisor's ideas are important.

Hold your fire

If you are upset by something your boss said, the tendency is to ignore the rest of the message and concentrate on your rebuttal. Sometimes, by listening to the remainder of your supervisor's message, your need for rebuttal will be eliminated. Do not interrupt or make assumptions about your manager's message.

Hear what is said

People often fail to understand what is said, even if they hear it directly, because they hear only what they want to hear. They employ selective listening.

You may listen more selectively to a problem boss to validate your dislike and their lack of competence. By hearing and retaining only what you want to hear, you may be filtering out critical information.

Work at listening

Listening is hard work and most of us have never been formally trained to do it. To be a good listener, you must be an active participant. Keep in mind that if you rearrange the letters in the word 'listen', you get 'silent'. You cannot listen when you are talking.

Exercise 4. Personal action plan for better communication

I have problems listening to or comprehending what my manager says for the following reasons:

_____

_____

_____

These are the ways I plan to increase my listening and comprehension effectiveness:

_____

_____

_____

_____

_____

_____

_____

Understanding takes two things:

talking and listening.
When we talk, we open the way for others
into our private thoughts and feelings,
and when we listen,
we step through the door
into another person's point of view.
Talking and listening –
with them come understanding.
And with understanding can come
some of life's most important things –
respect and acceptance and love.

Unknown

CHAPTER 4

Talk's Not Cheap: Building Bridges via Meetings

The basic ingredients needed for effective communication are expression, comprehension and listening. You can use those concepts to build a more effective partnership with your boss. Meetings are effective methods to build bridges of understanding.

We communicate for four basic reasons:

1. To build relationships
2. To express feelings
3. To exchange information so we can do our jobs, achieve goals and learn
4. To persuade, inspire and motivate others.

Exercise 1. Why we communicate
Think about the times you have communicated with your boss and your role in each of those situations. Then answer the following questions:

Which was more important – to express information well or be a good comprehender/listener, or both? Why?

_____

_____

_____

_____

_____

In which situations is it difficult to communicate effectively with your boss?

_____

_____

_____

_____

We need different skills to communicate different needs. Knowing which skills to use and when to use them is helpful.

Let's talk!

One of the best ways to elicit the information you need to do your job and increase your team's effectiveness is to have regularly scheduled private meetings between you and your boss, in addition to regularly scheduled staff meetings. These meetings can improve communication between you and your boss, resolve problems and increase partnership accountability.

In a study conducted at the University of Colorado Graduate School of Business Administration, regular manager–employee meetings had a positive effect on the organisational climate, team effectiveness and productivity. Participants in the study cited not just increased quantity of time with their supervisor, but improved quality of supervisor–employee communication. Naturally, the trust level between supervisor and employees also improved, because regularly addressing conflict prevented problems from growing.

Before you jump in . . .

Before you suggest a fortnightly or weekly meeting with your manager, prepare a list of reasons and benefits for having this meeting. You may have to sell your supervisor on this idea. The reasons and benefits discovered in the Colorado study may fit your particular partnership. Tick those that apply to your situation:

Reasons for fortnightly meetings

_____ To discuss administrative or organisational problems and suggestions for resolutions

_____ To resolve any interpersonal problems between you and your boss before they create more difficulties

_____ To discuss personal problems faced by either person that may impede your job

_____ To identify individual or organisational issues

_____ To provide an opportunity for mini-training sessions in administrative, technical and management skills. To prepare you for promotion opportunities or temporary supervisory responsibilities (in your manager's absence)

_____ To share information about what is happening in the organisation

_____ To set short- and long-term goals

_____ To review action items from previous meetings.

Benefits of fortnightly meetings

_____ Positive effect on team morale

_____ Will hold everyone accountable; therefore more assignments will be completed on time

_____ Improved quantity and quality of boss–employee communication

_____ Time savings and fewer interruptions

_____ Improved trust between boss and employee

_____ Quality of weekly staff meetings improves because meetings now concentrate on matters involving the entire staff versus individual staff members

_____ Fewer problems because conflicts are addressed regularly, preventing problems from growing.

Getting started

To have an effective meeting, prepare and use an agenda. Without it, the meeting can turn into a complaints session or social hour. Eventually, both you and your supervisor should create an agenda together. Initially, until your boss realises the benefits of the meeting, you may have to develop the agenda.

Meetings can be short, but they must be held regularly. To use the time most effectively, limit the discussion for each agenda item and allow no interruptions. You may want to hold your meeting in a conference room without a phone, or in your office where you can make arrangements to have the phone calls diverted. Time is wasted when meetings are interrupted, because it takes twice as long to overcome the interruption than to endure it.

When an organisation is in crisis, meetings should be more frequent and brief. For example, hospital staff would benefit from two short daily meetings, rather than one long meeting, so they can cope with the minute-to-minute crises in their environment.

Below is a specimen fortnightly meeting outline used by a sales manager with her boss.

Sample fortnightly meeting outline

1. **'Good news' reports.** Both employee and boss have one minute to share some good news about the past two weeks. It can be either business-related or personal. Good news reports get the meeting off to a positive start and get both parties involved. *Example.* 'Both sales reps met their quota for the second week in a row.'

2. **Business update.** Update each other on profits, losses, forthcoming sales incentive programmes, etc. Discuss business or competition news. This is where most other agenda items would fall.

3. **Problem solving.** Discuss administrative or organisational problems and suggestions for resolutions. Discuss any interpersonal or individual problems that are getting in the way.

4. **Fortnightly priorities.** Each person should go over his or

her two-week goals and any special projects he or she is working on. Realign priorities and set short- and long-term goals.

5. **Next meeting's agenda items.** Ask what the boss would like to discuss at your next meeting and create the new agenda.

Sample agenda

Fortnightly meeting – (date)		Time
1. Good news reports	both	2 min
2. Business update		
—Review action plan from previous meeting	Carla	10 min
—Forthcoming exhibitions	Chris	5 min
—Sales report	Carla	10 min
—Procedure overview	Chris	15 min
3. Problem solving		
—Sales reps' tickler system	Carla	10 min
—Missing call-backs	Chris	5 min
4. Fortnightly priorities	both	10 min
5. Action plan	Carla	5 min
6. Next meeting's agenda	both	3 min

Getting action from fortnightly meetings

To make your fortnightly meetings effective, you may need to follow them up with a memo. Many companies have found the Meeting Action Plan useful. You may want to try it, too.

The high cost of meetings

This simple formula can help you to work out how much one of your regular meetings costs your organisation.

Exercise 2. The high cost of meetings

1. List a weekly/monthly meeting _____

2. Time preparing for meeting   ____

MEETING ACTION PLAN

Meeting Date/Time: _____

Leader: _____ Recorder: _____

Action to be taken	Person responsible	Deadline completed
_____		
_____		
_____		
_____		
_____		
_____		
_____		
_____		
_____		
_____		

Time meeting started: _____ Ended: _____ Length: _____

Next meeting scheduled (Date): _____

Time begin: _____ End: _____

---

3. Time attending the meeting   + _____

                        Subtotal   _____

4. Number of attendees   _____

5. Multiply 3 (subtotal) × 4   = _____

6. Multiply 4 × average hourly wage £   = _____

                  Average cost of meeting   £ _____

Exercise 3. Examining the effectiveness of meetings
Assess the meetings that you attend regularly. Consider costs as well as problems that need attention.

1. List the regular meetings that you attend. How would you rate their effectiveness on a scale of 1 to 5 (1 = very ineffective, a total waste of my time, to 5 = very effective)?

   Meeting   **Rating**

   _____

   _____

2. What are the major problems with the meetings you attend?

   _____

   _____

3. What have you done to increase the effectiveness of those meetings?

   _____

   _____

If your boss is the meeting leader

If your boss is the meeting leader and you cannot avoid the meeting, you may be able to forestall some difficulties. Here are some suggestions.

1. **Problem**. No agenda

   Solutions. Suggest privately to your manager that agendas can speed up meetings and increase their productivity and effectiveness. Provide a sample agenda and, if necessary, assist in developing this one.

   Volunteer to take notes on the action plan. Once the group is committed to the idea and can see the benefits, rotate that responsibility.

Volunteer to explain the benefits and purpose of the agenda at the first meeting where it is implemented.

2. **Problem.** Meetings consistently overrun scheduled time

   Solutions. Suggest schedulng the meeting before lunch, before another engagement or before closing time. Most people will not allow a meeting to run into their personal time.

   Ask that time frames be assigned to each agenda item. Volunteer to be the official timekeeper so that no one goes over their time. Rotate this responsibility once the group can see and appreciate the benefits of doing so.

3. **Problem.** Speakers ramble

   Solutions. When the speaker stops for breath, rephrase one of the statements and make a comment to get back on track. Ask for someone else's opinion. Ask your boss if the group can move on to the next agenda item.

   Refer to the agenda, and ask which topic the speaker is discussing. Say, 'I'm sorry, but I'm a little lost. How is this related to the topic?'

4. **Problem.** Interruptions

   Solutions. Discuss privately with the meeting leader how attendance can be limited only to the most appropriate people and explain the benefits of keeping the participants to a minimum.

   Volunteer to facilitate the meeting. Tell the group you will start the meeting on time and then do it.

   Suggest holding a 'stand up' meeting, if appropriate.

   Discuss the interruption problem during the meeting. As a group, define what constitutes an emergency and when the group should allow interruptions. Put a message board outside the meeting room so the group can check for messages at breaks. Get the group to commit themselves to allowing no interruptions. One organisation scheduled 15-minute breaks every hour to allow for this.

Exercise 4. Meeting action ideas

Create your own action plan for more efficient meetings. Return to Exercise 3 and jot down major problems with the meetings you attend:

_____

_____

_____

What will you do to increase the effectiveness of those meetings?

_____

_____

_____

_____

_____

_____

CHAPTER 5
Confronting with Compassion

Criticising anyone, especially your supervisor, is difficult and requires sensitivity. However, if you can learn this art, your working life may improve. Criticism can uncover problems early, which can lead to early solutions and save time. If correctly handled, criticism encourages both the critic and the one criticised – even bosses – to learn and grow.

How can you criticise your manager?

Examine your attitude towards giving criticism and some of the pitfalls you may encounter.

Exercise 1. Criticism pitfalls
Tick the attitudes you have that inhibit your giving criticism:

_____ If I wait long enough, the situation will probably resolve itself, so I do not have to get involved.

_____ Since I do not like to receive criticism, I cannot imagine my supervisor would; therefore, I choose to ignore the problem.

_____ I criticise indirectly by using sarcasm or jokes.

_____ I would rather complain to my colleagues than criticise my manager directly.

_____ There never seems to be a right time to criticise, and I keep putting off giving criticism.

_____ It takes so much time to criticise effectively; I would rather do more work than take the time to give feedback to my supervisor.

_____ I am unsure of how my manager will respond to my criticism; therefore, I avoid giving it.

_____ I am not perfect, and my boss has so much more experience than I do; who am I to judge my supervisor's behaviour?

_____ If I give my boss negative feedback, it may be used against me at my next performance evaluation.

_____ I have let the situation go on for too long now, and I am so angry that I am sure I'm going to blow up and mishandle the situation.

The more of these attitudes you ticked, the more difficulty you will have criticising anyone, particularly your boss.

Criticising your boss

One study found that people without supervisory responsibilities found it more difficult to criticise than those who have them. More people (51 per cent) find it difficult to criticise their boss, and regardless of whom they criticise, find that getting started is the most difficult part.

Some people ignore problematic situations and hope that if they wait long enough the problem will disappear. Avoiding the situation may be appropriate when the issue is trivial or if the problem is symptomatic of even more pressing problems. However, ignoring a situation is inappropriate most of the time because most problems do not go away on their own; they usually escalate.

Some people refuse to criticise for fear their boss will not like them or may give them a negative performance review. Criticising your boss may result in conflict, but avoiding conflict at all costs will not solve the problem either.

Because many people are uncomfortable receiving feedback, we are reluctant to give it. This contradicts most research conducted on motivation, which suggests that feedback is one of the biggest motivators for change. Even bosses can appreciate well thought-out feedback and criticism.

Providing negative feedback or criticism to your boss can be very delicate. People have been known to cheat, lie and kill to save face. Neither forget nor underestimate your boss's need to preserve his or her reputation and dignity.

Exercise 2. Criticism analysis
Before you criticise your boss, consider the specifics of your criticism, as well as your motives. Complete the following analysis:

1. Describe the situation and problem you are experiencing with your boss.

   _____

   _____

   _____

2. When did this problem start, and what is the impact on you?

   _____

   _____

   _____

3. How do you think your boss will react to your criticism? What are the risks involved in providing this feedback?

   _____

   _____

   _____

4. What are the benefits to you if this problem is resolved?

   _____

   _____

   _____

5. Do the benefits far outweigh the costs? Yes/No/Not sure (Explain)

   _____

   _____

   _____

If you answered 'No' to the last question, the costs are too high. You will probably not want to criticise your supervisor. You might want to think through other options for coping with this situation. If your answer is 'Yes' or you are not sure, the five Ss of providing unsolicited feedback will help you to criticise your boss:

Five Ss of providing unsolicited feedback

Step 1. Select your timing
Timing is critical. If your boss is under considerable stress, wait for a better time. Pick the time and place carefully to avoid interruptions or distractions. Set an appointment rather than dropping in so that your boss senses the importance of the discussion.

Step 2. Secure the boss's permission
Tell your supervisor you have something that will help both of you to become more effective. Don't negate the information by saying, 'It's really not that big a deal, but . . .' Say, 'I think I have some information that would be helpful to our team. Could we schedule a meeting so that we can discuss my ideas?'

Do not skip over your boss and take your problems to your boss's supervisor. Bypassing your manager leaves you with little credibility, even if your points are valid ones. Also, do not criticise your supervisor publicly or to your colleagues; it is unprofessional and unacceptable behaviour.

Step 3. Share specifics
Get your facts straight. If you cannot provide specific examples of the problems you are discussing, your boss will probably dismiss your comments. An effective formula for giving criticism to your manager is the DASS script described on the next page.

The DASS script

This is how a DASS script works:

Describe: (the exact behaviour you find bothersome) 'When you . . .'

Acknowledge: (what you really feel about the manager's behaviour or situation) 'I feel . . .'

Specify: (ask for a different, specified behaviour) 'What I would prefer . . .'

Show team benefits: (what is in it for the manager and the team) 'This is how you will benefit . . .'

DASS script examples

Poor version	Better version
Describe 'You never start and end staff meetings on time.'	'When we end staff meetings late, I am late for my next appointment.'
Acknowledge 'You make me so angry I could scream.'	'I feel frustrated and rushed for the rest of the day.'
Specify 'Why don't you learn how to manage?'	'I would prefer that we should set a realistic finishing time for our staff meetings.'
Show team benefits	'That way we could all make better use of our time after the meeting and increase our productivity and time effectiveness.'

We often omit the action-oriented *specify* step. A part of us really wants an apology from the other person after we tell him or her how we feel. One of the most important steps in criticising people is specifying actions they can take. Then the other person can do something about the criticism, rather than defensively react to our disclosure of negative feelings. Offer to help if you can.

Step 4. Show team benefits
Show your boss the benefits that will accrue to the entire team by a change of behaviour. You want to build up, not pull down, your boss.

Step 5. Summarise your agreement
Summarise what has been discussed and confirm your mutual commitment. Show enthusiasm for the plans made. Be positive. Show your willingness and interest in improving yourself. Each time you work with your boss or are completing a project, ask, 'How could I have improved my performance?'

Give your boss an opportunity to make other suggestions. Close the discussion on a friendly, upbeat note. 'I really appreciate your willingness to discuss this and I am confident our team is going to benefit from these changes. Thank you.'

Exercise 3. Providing unsolicited feedback to your boss
Complete the following action plan on giving unsolicited criticism to your boss. Choose a specific criticism you wish to give.

Step 1. Select your timing. When is the best time to criticise your boss?

_____

_____

_____

Step 2. Secure their permission. How are you going to gain their permission?

_____

_____

_____

Step 3. Share specifics. Using the DASS script, jot down your thoughts. Describe (the behaviour you find bothersome):
'When you . . . _____'

Acknowledge (what you feel):
'I feel . . . _____'

Specify (ask for a different, specified behaviour):
'What I would prefer . . . _____'

Show team benefits:
'I really appreciate your interest and know that this will positively affect our team by . . ._____.'

'Thanks!'

CHAPTER 6

How to Read Your Boss

Even the best efforts of competent employees are hindered if they do not have information about their particular boss's needs, preferences, motivators and demotivators. As a result, supervisors may perceive their staff as resistant, incapable, disloyal, uncooperative or even incompetent. Employees may perceive their supervisor as unpredictable, unclear or uncaring.

Exercise 1. Complaints and frustrations
Following is a list of common complaints expressed by people who do not understand their managers. Tick the statements that characterise your frustrations with your supervisor.

_____ My boss thrives on chaos that she/he creates.
_____ I never complete an assignment because of all the last minute revisions and rewrites.
_____ My boss talks so much during staff meetings that we never get out on time and we adjourn with the agenda only partially completed.
_____ My manager is so specific about how I should do my work that there really is no room for creativity.
_____ My supervisor is so cautious about making changes that it is impossible to get a timely decision.
_____ Our team starts a project and then our manager gives us five more things to do.
_____ By rushing and neglecting details, my boss creates crises that I have to resolve.

____ My supervisor is always distracted. Even while we are discussing a project, he takes telephone calls and deals with people who drop in to ask questions.

____ Other (specify) _____

_____

_____

Many working styles can be accommodated in a comfortable relationship, but balance and initiative are necessary. If the employee respects an employer's need for speedy communication, in all likelihood the employer will reciprocate by respecting the employee's need for more information. Usually the employee must act first.

Reading your boss

Everyone has predictable behavioural patterns. As you learn why people behave in certain ways, you will learn to communicate better. The READ method* can increase your boss–observation skills. The steps are:

R = Review the signs
E = Evaluate established patterns
A = Apply appropriate approach
D = Do something daily

Step 1. R = Review
Working with your boss every day is like driving to work every day. After taking the same route many times, the driver does not pay much attention to the road. So it is with employer and worker. They may endlessly repeat the same practices and wonder why nothing ever improves or changes.

Exercise 2. The STOP sign
Pause to read the stop signs along the way. They could signal

---

*The READ terminology is derived from the *Personal Profile System*, published by Carlson Learning Company.

danger or provide alternative directions. Tick at least three behaviour patterns that describe your boss's actions.

Typical behaviour	Your boss

1. Carefully plans everything with lists, short- and long-range plans, deadlines. **P**____
2. Seeks perfection in everything; researches every decision. **P**____
3. Performs routine work and follows schedules such as starting and ending work at the same time every day. **S**____
4. Experiments with new ideas and projects; takes risks with proven projects. **T**____
5. Tells people what to do more than asking or persuading them. **T**____
6. Is very outgoing and friendly, smiles a lot, knows about everyone at work. **O**____
7. Is very low key; can be depended on to get work done. **S**____
8. Focuses on end result or goals rather than processes used to get there. **T**____
9. Asks questions such as 'How do people work together? Do they enjoy their work?' **O**____
10. Often gives detailed directions on how to carry out a new assignment. **S**____
11. Asks, 'What is the bottom line, end result or the big picture?' **T**____
12. Enquires when evaluating an assignment, 'Where is the research on this? How can I be sure it will work?' **P**____
13. When stressed, becomes disorganised and talks a lot. **O**____
14. Office and desk are very neatly organised; has an efficient filing system. **S**____
15. When communicating with people, is encouraging, supportive, asks their opinions, lets others handle details. **O**____
16. Communicates precisely based on facts, logic, proven ideas rather than feelings and assumptions. **P**____

Now count how many times you ticked each letter and write it below.

Number ticked

S_____
T_____
O_____
P_____

The highest numbers represent behaviour patterns that your supervisor uses most of the time. Stop to think about them. Once you understand these patterns, you can adjust your behaviour to improve communications.

The diagram on page 58 explains how to evaluate established behavioural patterns.

STOP	
Overall description	**Approach**
Supervisors with these behaviours are most likely to:	*The best way to work effectively with this boss is to:*
S Avoid surprises. Work/communicate well in a **T** small group. Work steadily on routine tasks. **E** Stay neat and organised. Need detailed directions. **A** Have difficulty in an unclear, changing situation. **D** **Y**	Be patient. Ask questions and listen. Be quiet and non-confrontational. Give time to adjust and respond. Emphasise approaches that will minimise risk. Plan action steps. Stay organised yourself. Do not make sudden or drastic changes. Be dependable. Give specific details. Work as part of the team.
T Act with self-confidence **R** Prefer variety and challenges **E** to a routine job. **N** Be very willing to experiment **D** and set new trends. Take risks and assume leader- **S** ship roles. **E** Be competitive and **T** controlling. **T** Create chaos with new **E** ventures. **R**	Communicate briefly and directly. If they move recklessly, show how you can help them to reach goals faster and better. Be positive. Focus on results, limit details to essentials. Be willing to experiment. Value their innovation. Do not slow them down too much or tell them what to do.

Step 2. E = Evaluate established patterns

On the left is a description of each of four behaviour patterns represented by the stop sign. On the right is the matching approach most likely to be successful with that behaviour.

STOP	
Overall description	**Approach**

O Communicate easily with
 U   many people.
 T Prefer flexibility, little
 G   control by others.
 O Respond well to recognition
 I   and value helping people.
 N Lose focus and waste time
 G   with too much talking.
	Be friendly, enthusiastic.
	 Listen.
	 Provide opportunities to help
	    people.
	 Organise details, paperwork,
	    scheduling.
	 Be flexible.
	 Value their understanding of
	    people.
	 Include them in discussions,
	    committees, high-profile
	    projects.

P Want everything to be done
 E   correctly, in compliance
 R   with laws, standards,
 F   policies and procedures.
 E Dislike chaos or unpredictable
 C   working environment.
 T Expect themselves and others
 I   to be experts.
 O Become over-critical and
 N   demanding of themselves
 I   and others.
 S
 T
	Patiently provide lots of data.
	 Research facts first,
	    especially if idea departs
	    from established practice.
	 Use strategic planning and
	    statistical information.
	 Value their expertise.
	 Help them to make timely
	    decisions.
	 Do outstanding work.
	 Be diplomatic and logical.

Step 3. A = Apply appropriate approach

Now we will take each of the four behavioural patterns and demonstrate how to apply the STOP, READ and DASS guidelines (see Chapter 5 for DASS script).

S Steadies sometimes have difficulty coping with unusual situations. They prefer to follow established patterns and make changes gradually.

Appropriate approach. Find out what kind of information your boss needs, and identify timelines. Use a friendly, unrushed manner and tone of voice. Suggest ways to minimise risks.

Say, 'When my recommendations for improving my department are delayed, it means everyone will have to rush at the last minute. I would prefer to make changes more promptly. I would like to discuss a gradual change in the following procedures_____. I have assessed the possible problems and have proposed solutions. What other information would you need to reach a decision? Have I left out anything that you might see as a potential problem if we make this change? I'd like to have a response within a month so we can avoid the next crisis.'

T **Trend setters** are willing to experiment, they like variety, and they like to take risks. Sometimes they create so much change that employees feel they are working in a chaotic environment.

Appropriate approach. Focus on results and ask for priorities. Offer to help make the new ventures successful.

A possible script: 'When expectations change constantly, it is hard for me to keep up. I feel overwhelmed. What I would prefer is to develop an overall plan and deadlines. I would be happy to help in any way possible, such as keeping track of deadlines and coordinating our team. We could get others to help out and we would not be in crisis all the time.'

O **Outgoing** people enjoy conversations and lose track of time easily. They are committed to the democratic process and want people to feel involved and appreciated.

Appropriate approach. 'I enjoy the chance to talk during staff meetings. You really have a talent for bringing people out.

However, I feel frustrated that we can't get through the entire agenda. We run late and then I'm late for my next appointment. Maybe we could socialise for about 15 minutes at the beginning and again at the end. I could help as timekeeper for the agenda. Then we would cover everything and could plan our day better.'

P **Perfectionists** always find a better way to do something, and they have trouble knowing when to stop. They have high expectations for themselves and others.

Appropriate approach. Ask more questions in advance and be sure to agree on outcomes, action steps and a timetable. Clarify how much detail and data are required in advance. Several midpoint progress checks would be helpful.

Say, 'When I have to rewrite reports, it is difficult to keep up with the deadlines. I feel confused about my role, and I'm not sure if the quality of my work is satisfactory. I'd prefer us to clarify expectations in advance. I could develop an outline for your review. Then we could review the report at agreed checkpoints. If we work like this, it will reduce rewrites and wasted time.'

CHAPTER 7

The Care and Feeding of a Boss

Bosses value many qualities in their employees. In addition to shared professional goals, managers want to see evidence of personal initiative and good thinking skills. Managers from organisations such as banking, manufacturing, education, social service agencies and museums say the following abilities are important to them.

- Decision-making
- Responsibility
- Communication
- Creativity
- Quality
- Time management

Six ways to become a star

You can become a 'star employee' by exhibiting the above qualities. Make a commitment to gain these qualities by completing the following exercise.

Exercise 1.
Tick each of the following abilities that you intend to improve on in the next six months:

☐ **1. Decision-making**
   Although I may occasionally err, I will take a risk rather than do nothing. I will not sit around waiting for someone to tell me what to do. If I see a job that needs to be done, I will do it.

☐ **2. Responsibility**
I will be where I am supposed to be and take responsibility for my actions. I will be willing to work hard, even if it involves overtime. I will get my job done without constant checking and nagging, follow through on my own and tie up loose ends.

☐ **3. Communication**
I will be patient, willing to listen and work at getting along with customers, colleagues and managers. If the boss does something helpful, I will say so. I will provide verbal affirmation without being manipulative. I will go directly to my boss for discussion about problems, rather than complain to other members of staff.

☐ **4. Creativity**
I will be flexible and open to change. I will study problems from a different perspective. I will channel my innovative ideas to produce improvement rather than chaos or policy violations.

☐ **5. Quality**
I will deliver services and products with distinction to external and internal customers. I will complete my work so colleagues can do theirs properly. I will use my knowledge and job skills with personal pride. I will be willing to improve my own knowledge and skills, learn to understand the company 'big picture' and help to create it.

☐ **6. Time management**
I will control unnecessary interruptions in my own work and in interactions with others. I will not waste my boss's time. I will be on time for meetings and lunch. I will meet project deadlines and return telephone calls promptly.

Successful employee actions

Different companies rank star qualities differently, depending on company culture, personal preferences, the nature of the work and the employee's skill and knowledge. However, some general practices will put you ahead anywhere.

Keep your boss informed

Keeping your boss informed demonstrates at least two of the six abilities: responsibility and communication. Managers from many organisational levels consistently list several areas where they want to be kept informed:

1. **Progress on projects**
   Be accountable to your boss on all assigned projects by following through without being reminded. Update your boss regularly on your progress and potential delays.

2. **Assignment completion**
   Tell your boss when you finish an assignment and ask for feedback. If you consistently ask for feedback, there should be no surprises at your performance review.

3. **Anticipated problems**
   If you anticipate a delay for any reason, inform your boss. Confront a problem at once so it does not escalate. Your boss may have ideas for how you can work around those problems. Do not cover up your mistakes. It is more difficult to explain why you hid the mistake than why you made it.

Monthly status report

Many employees have found that submitting a monthly status report is helpful in communicating problems. Although status reports take time, they are effective in keeping your boss informed and creating a record of what you have done, which can be helpful for performance evaluations or job interviews.

Exercise 2. Sample monthly status report

Monthly status report

Name_____Date_____

1. Completed assignments:
   A)_____

   B)_____

   C)_____

   D)_____

2. Status on current projects:
   A)_____

   B)_____

   C)_____

   D)_____

3. Anticipated problems or concerns:

   _____

   _____

Turn complaints into proposals

When you are reporting a concern or problem, always be prepared with solutions. Bosses love to see initiative and problem-solving skills in their employees. This is a simple way to show what you can do. You may want to write your ideas down so your boss can read them. Written reports have two advantages: they put the decision-making back into the boss's lap and they can be given to a higher authority so you can receive credit for your ideas. Ask if your boss prefers a combination of oral and written reports.

Exercise 3. Turning complaints into proposals

Turning negatives to positives demonstrates one of the star abilities: creativity. Think of a complaint that you would like your boss to take action on and use the following sample complaint proposal form to put your thoughts in writing.

Complaint proposal form

1. Problem area:_____

2. Potential causes:_____

3. Solutions:_____

4. Recommended solution and rationale:_____

5. Implementation strategy (Who, When, Where):_____

   _____

6. Progress checkpoint (date to check on strategy effectiveness):

   _____

   _____

Praising upwards

Bosses need to know they are doing a good job. Many studies indicate that feedback is the prime motivator, yet upper level managers often do not receive any more feedback than you do. Providing feedback effectively demonstrates your star abilities of communication and creativity.

If you want to praise your boss, keep it specific and sincere. The story is told of the employee who said to his boss, 'You are the best boss a person could ever have. Every night I go home and tell my wife how great you are and how much I enjoy working for you.' Nobody will believe that.

Praise example

Your boss gives you a copy of the minutes from her management staff meeting. You might say (*be specific*), 'Mary, I appreciate your providing me with a copy of your management staff meeting minutes. (*Be sincere*) I find it extremely helpful to know how my projects fit in with the larger departmental aims. By seeing the big picture, I can target the information I provide you with. Thanks for keeping me so well informed.'

How much do you want to bet that Mary will continue to give her employee copies of her minutes? Praise encourages us to continue that same behaviour.

Things bosses don't want

In addition to understanding what abilities and behaviour your employer and organisation find desirable, it is just as important to know what is unacceptable.

Exercise 4. Undesirable behaviour
The following is a list of employee behaviours that many managers find unacceptable. Tick those that you believe it is important to avoid.

_____ 1. To embarrass, surprise or confront one's supervisor publicly
_____ 2. To say nothing or to complain to other people when angry, depressed, demoralised or confused about work
_____ 3. To gossip and spread unfounded rumours
_____ 4. To attempt a 'palace coup', that is, to attempt to remove the boss from his or her position
_____ 5. To engage in undercover sabotage and to demoralise others
_____ 6. To steal time, property, information or ideas
_____ 7. Other (specify)_____

Most people enjoy an opportunity to rate themselves so they

can identify areas for self-improvement. The following survey will help you to assess whether you do things that your boss or organisation does not find acceptable.

Exercise 5. Assess yourself
Respond by ticking 'Yes' or 'No'. Be honest with yourself.

	Yes	No
1. Do you usually have difficulty making decisions at work?	☐	☐
2. Are most of your decisions good?	☐	☐
3. Are you willing to stay at work after closing time if a job is not completed?	☐	☐
4. Do you follow your organisation's rules and directives?	☐	☐
5. Do you complain rarely and then only to your immediate supervisor?	☐	☐
6. Are you willing to accept responsibility for your mistakes?	☐	☐
7. Do you work hard at getting on with other workers and supervisors?	☐	☐
8. Are you friendly yet task-oriented at work?	☐	☐
9. Do you try to do your best at work?	☐	☐
10. Do you tend to put things off and do them at the last minute?	☐	☐

Give yourself one point for a 'No' response on questions 1 and 10, and one point for each 'Yes' response on items 2–9. Scores of 9 and 10 are outstanding. Most employers would be delighted to have you working for them. Scores of 7 or 8 are above average. Your boss should consider you a valuable employee. A little improvement and you could be outstanding. Scores of 4 to 6 are within the average range. You and your boss would benefit from collaborative communication. Scores under 4 are below average. You need major changes on your job, or a new one.

Once you have assessed any undesirable behaviour, you can make improvements.

Exercise 6. Make improvements

List the most critical questions from Exercise 5. Describe why the questions you ticked may be a problem, and list changes you wish to make. An example is provided.

Action example	
Question number	**Reason and action steps**
1	*Reason.* I have trouble making decisions because my boss changes her mind frequently.
	Action. Try to get written directions even if I write them. Then, check on progress frequently to be sure I am on the right track.

Question number	**Reason and action steps**
_____	*Reason:* _____
	_____
	Action: _____
	_____
_____	*Reason:* _____
	_____
	Action: _____
	_____
_____	*Reason:* _____
	_____
	Action: _____
	_____

CHAPTER 8
Managing Time-Management Monsters

All over the world, companies are merging and laying off employees. The problem for the remaining staff is how to get all the necessary work done. How do we cope with multiple priorities and multiple bosses? What do we do with a boss who is disorganised? Time is what we want the most and what we make the worst use of.

Productivity principles

Before you can build a solid partnership with your supervisor, you need to concentrate on some basic productivity principles. Some people claim that planning takes all the sport out of life – yet the key to managing time effectively is planning so that your goals come to fruition. Some claim that unless we invest 1 per cent of each project's time-span on planning, the project will take 2.7 times longer to complete. We will now examine the basic steps of time management.

Planning steps

1. **Analyse the situation.** Set goals according to your own values and purpose, within the framework of the organisation. Your goals should also meet your supervisor's goals. Set up a three- to five-year plan and break it down into achievable one-year plans. Ask yourself, 'What do I need to do this year (month, week) to get closer to achieving my long-range goals?'

2. **Develop weekly objectives.** Establish short-range goals that will lead you to your long-range plans.

3. **Make decisions on priority items and develop a daily plan.** Prioritise according to your and the organisation's goals. You may want to use an ABCD system (or whatever system works for you).

> **A** = Important (goal-related) and urgent
> **B** = Important, but not urgent
> **C** = Urgent, but not important
> **D** = Neither important nor urgent

Once you have made a list of what needs to be done, prioritise it, using your system, and estimate how long each item will take. Continually rearrange your schedule so that you do the most important things first; block out large chunks of time for the really important tasks.

Sometimes everything becomes an A priority, and we begin living from crisis to crisis. Do not do whatever screams the loudest unless it is important. Learn to say 'no'. Focus on the B tasks, which will give the biggest pay-off. Constantly remind yourself of your goals and ask yourself what you have done today to get one step closer to them.

4. **Stick to your plan and review the results.** It will probably take about 30 days of concentrated effort to get your plan to work for you. Most people who stick to it for several months really get hooked and cannot imagine what they did before they used it.

Planning is not the only ingredient in effective time management. Many barriers can restrict effective time management in boss–employee partnerships.

Barrier 1
Interruptions

Generally, 80 per cent of your interruptions come from 20 per cent of the people. What if that 20 per cent is your boss? Here are some ideas for limiting interruptions:

1. Hold fortnightly meetings with your boss. Think strategically of ways to minimise your boss's interruptions.
2. Hold stand-up meetings. This eliminates unnecessary socialising. Do not sit down when you go into your boss's office for a quick question.
3. If your boss comes into your office frequently and takes up too much of your time, stand up immediately or maintain your working posture: keep your hands on the keyboard. Tell your boss diplomatically that it is not a good time to interrupt.

   Use interruption times to delegate upwards. Ask your boss for help. Do not ask them if they stopped by for a particular reason. That will merely prolong the interruption. If it was important, they will let you know.
4. Be assertive – learn to say 'no'. It is particularly difficult to say not to your boss. It must be done with tact and diplomacy so your behaviour will not reflect negatively on your performance evaluation.

Saying no to your boss
Before you say no to your supervisor, make sure you are using your support staff and other team members to the full. Some people might not be as swamped as you are. Ask them for help. Develop support staff so that you can delegate more work. Then things can get done even when you are not there.

When you say no to your boss:

- Acknowledge the boss's request. Be sure you understand it.
- Give the reason why you cannot; negotiate.
- Provide alternatives.

For example, if your boss asks you to photocopy a report, say that you would be happy to (acknowledge request), but you are at a critical step on project xyz (give reason). Should you stop working on project xyz, or could your boss wait for the copies until tomorrow (provide alternative)?

Negotiate with your boss. When you are asked to do something, first find out the resources (staff and money) that will be available, the level of authority you will have, what kind of feedback you can expect and project deadlines. Once you have said no, anticipate that your boss will come back with a stronger plea for help. Refuse again with the same reason so that your manager senses your honesty and firmness about the situation.

5. Rearrange your office so that you are not facing the open door and cannot catch people's eyes as they go by. Remove guest chairs.
6. Discuss with your boss the idea of establishing a quiet time – a known period where you accept no interruptions or phone calls. This is work time to be guarded preciously. It is very important for you to return phone calls and messages when using this system so that people do not feel compelled to interrupt you.
7. If you have your own office, close your door and put up a notice that says, 'Please do not interrupt. I will be available at (time).' Put a notepad on your door so people can leave messages.

   If you are in an open plan office, use a flag system to let people know when you are not to be interrupted. A green flag means 'interrupt me if necessary', yellow is 'enter with caution' and a red flag means 'enter only in an emergency'.
8. Use team logs. Set up a sheet of paper or folder for each key person you work with. When you think of something to ask them, ask yourself, 'Can this wait?' If it can, enter it on their team log sheet. If it cannot wait, interrupt them. If your supervisor interrupts you, ask him/her the questions from your team log. At an agreed time, go over each other's team logs.

Sample team log

Date _____ Name of key person _____

— Confirm project meeting timetable and location
— Ask about new personnel policy application to our department
— Computer sales person desires meeting – interested?
— Lunch meeting with client Smith is cancelled for next Tuesday

---

9. Have visitors screened by a third party. Set up call-back periods and return all your calls at once.
10. Set time limits on meetings.

Barrier 2
Changing priorities

When you do not know what your priorities are, or your boss changes priorities frequently, you may become frustrated and feel a lack of accomplishment from your job. There are a couple of things you can do.

When your boss changes priorities ask 'How does this affect the course of direction we were on?' If there are no priorities, develop a sense of what the priorities should be, based on your knowledge of the organisation's goals and mission. Review your list, tell your boss what you are doing and ask for feedback. Be flexible. You may not see the big picture, so ask questions and seek feedback.

Barrier 3
Coping with multiple bosses

Multiple bosses can mean multiple directives. What can you do?

Always ask your bosses for deadlines and priority levels. Communicate immediately if there is a conflict. Let the bosses work out among themselves which is the most important task to complete. Offer alternatives when saying no. Alternatives include different time frames from those requested, suggestions for who else might be able to help out and where else the work might be handled. Ask the bosses to help you design a work order form, which will help you to determine priorities, manage the work flow and lessen interruptions. Different coloured paper could indicate the priority level of the requests.

Sample work order form

Today's date: _____ Requested by: _____

Time submitted: _____

Project/Item: _____

Return to me:　　□　Draft　　□　Final

Formatting space: □ Single　　□ Double　　□ Triple

Type of paper: _____

No of copies I need: _____

Send additional copies to the following: _____

Post:　□　Registered　□　First class　□　Second class

　　　　　　□　Hand deliver　　□　Fax

Work completed by: _____

Date: _____ Time _____

As long as the requests are not confidential, you can stack these work order forms on your desk in priority order. Then it is easy to point out to your boss(es), when a new request is made, what you are working on and where the new request fits in.

Barrier 4
Lack of information

Information is power and the lack of it greatly lessens your chance of doing an effective job. There are several ways you can try to gain access to information from your boss.

Tell your boss that you need the information. Be diplomatically aggressive – use meetings, the phone and memos to ask for the information. Be sincere. Share your feelings of frustration with your boss, and ask if there is anything you can do to get access to the information. Follow up when you do not hear from your boss. Put information items on the fortnightly meeting agenda. Plan ahead for slow response time. Use electronic mail to facilitate information sharing. Ask for a copy of your boss's management staff meeting minutes so that you can get a better sense of the big picture.

Put your project recommendations in writing and give a deadline date: 'If I do not hear from you by (date), I will proceed as outlined.'

Barrier 5
Unavailable boss

If your boss is never around, it means he or she trusts you. However, sometimes you need to see your boss. Take control and set time aside to meet.

Take your boss off-site, away from the telephone and other interruptions – the board room, a local restaurant or conference room might work. Never surprise your boss. Put things in writing, or use office technology including voice mail or electronic mail to leave and retrieve messages.

Build alliances with peers and secretaries. They may have more access to the boss and be willing to share information they have obtained. Discuss the problem with your boss and agree on a system to share information.

Barrier 6
Disorganised boss

Robert Half International surveyed executives and found they waste nearly four weeks a year because they cannot find things and another three weeks a year on unnecessary phone calls. So what can you do for your disorganised boss?

Keep a dated copy of everything you send to your boss. Help your boss to establish realistic time frames. Be flexible and use your energy to help alleviate the problem rather than escalate it. Share your frustration and confront the issue. If you are an organised assistant or the secretary, screen phone calls and interruptions. Suggest a daily quiet time. Try to anticipate your employer's needs; plan ahead. Try to understand the external factors that may be influencing your boss's organisational style. Recognise the different personality styles and how they affect time usage. Determine how you might minimise your boss's weaknesses as well as your own.

A final thought
Time is money. The only person who saves time is the one who spends it wisely in the first place. Better time management will help you and your boss to become more time-effective partners.

CHAPTER 9
Coping with Dreadful Bosses

A graduate psychology student of the US University of Tulsa conducted a two-year study about why bosses are unpopular with their employees. The study, presented to the American Psychological Association and reported in the *APA Monitor*, revealed that:

- The most stressful job aspect for 60 per cent of workers is their immediate supervisor.
- Many employees have spent a great deal of time working for what they consider a dreadful boss.

The researchers concluded from this study and others that 60 to 75 per cent of managers are incompetent.

All bosses are not created equal

Some bosses are a joy and a delight to work with. If you have one like this, count yourself blessed and give this person lots of positive feedback. However, even the best supervisor some-times engages in problem behaviour, especially when stress and tension are high.

A problem boss, on the other hand, can make life miserable for employees. Some workers 'fire' their bosses and move on to other opportunities; others develop techniques and strategies to cope with dreadful bosses.

The qualities you bring to a professional relationship can help to determine your relationship with your boss, including:

- Level of self-esteem and job experience
- Willingness to take risks and confront the boss
- Flexibility to change jobs or careers
- Dependency on company benefits: staff mortgage, company car, private medicine, retirement pension, etc.
- Value system
- Sense of humour and ability to depersonalise work relationships
- Behavioural style
- Time and energy for improving the relationship with your boss
- Satisfaction with the work itself compared to the amount of stress in the relationship
- Degree of open communication with your boss.

Because of our qualities, each of us will draw the line at what we consider to be dreadful at a different point. For example, one boss may be very demanding and tyrannical, but employees may find that he is also fair and honest. A person who has high self-esteem might not find this type of boss as difficult as someone who is sensitive and new to the job.

Intolerable boss behaviour

The first of the following two lists includes supervisory behaviour that some would find unacceptable. The second list includes strategies people have used to cope with them:

- **Personal quirks**
  This person may demonstrate exaggerated normal characteristics to the point of creating problems. For example, a commitment to quality work can lead to perfectionism; friendliness can lead to an exaggerated need to be liked, with consequent neglect of job tasks. Psychological problems such as depression, drug and alcohol abuse or mental disabilities can result in unpredictable behaviour.

- **Slave-driver bosses**
  A slave-driver supervisor may threaten, criticise and unreasonably demand work from employees. This boss may set unrealistically high expectations, not accept disagreement and use power and a biting tongue to dominate and manipulate employees.

- **Incompetent bosses**
  This boss cannot make a decision or may avoid contact with employees. This manager may cave in easily to pressure or change direction frequently and without warning. She/he does not know how to manage people.

The same boss may use a combination of intolerable behaviours and add a few twists. It is possible to have a slave-driver boss who also has personal quirks. On the other hand, a quirky manager may be competent in all other ways.

An important criterion to use in determining unacceptable boss behaviour is to consider the impact both on the individual employee and on the organisation as a whole.

What can you do?

- **No action**
  Continue to do your work. Bottle up feelings and accept pain caused by a negative and destructive supervisor. Take no action to improve the situation. Pause to observe and think before doing anything. *Taking no action will not put your job at risk, but it may greatly affect your productivity and health.*

- **Modify your own behaviour**
  Adjust your work style to the needs of your boss. Use better communication strategies. Adapt your behavioural style to your boss's needs regarding use of time, level of detail,

friendliness, change and perfectionism, etc. Change your responses (thoughts and feelings) to your boss's actions. This behaviour has a *low to moderate risk regarding loss of job, but has higher potential for job improvement.*

- **Manage your boss**
  Provide praise and criticism. Meet your boss privately to improve the situation. Meet in a group to develop agreement. This behaviour has a *moderate risk, because you must take the initiative. However, the potential for improvement is great.*

- **Oppose your boss**
  Openly criticise or confront your supervisor's unacceptable behaviour. Seek relief at the next level. Refuse to follow directives. Break company rules. This behaviour exposes you to a *high risk of losing your job; however, it may be necessary when the effect of your boss's behaviour is destructive.*

- **Fire your boss**
  Transfer within the company. Quietly seek alternative employment and leave. Leave without another job. This behaviour poses a *high risk to current employment and possibly to future employment. However, this step may become positive if done in a planned, rather than impulsive, manner.*

The problem is analysed on the next page.

Risk to action steps diagram

The diagram below illustrates the relationship between level of
risk and action steps. As the action steps move higher, the level
of risk also rises.

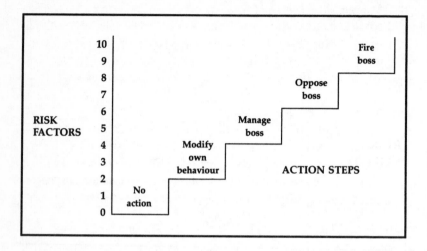

Scale 1
Level of risk
How do you know which strategy to match to which behaviour?
The choice is directly related to the level of risk you are willing
to assume and how severe you perceive the problem to be.

Exercise 1. How bad is it really?
Using the following scale, pinpoint your willingness to take
risks. The descriptions next to the scale suggest what a person
who exercises low, medium or high risk behaviour might do.
Make an x on the vertical line where you think your risk factors
are. (For example, if you feel that any action on your part
would endanger future employment, you will mark an x
between 0 and 3 on the vertical line.)

10	**High risk.** Completely open and direct about what I feel and think. Unafraid of negative consequences. Know I can get a better job,
9	probably with better pay. Do not feel locked in to benefits. Will leave if things get impossible.
8	
7	
6	

RISK FACTORS

	Medium risk. Can raise some issues and discuss some feelings and ideas. Carefully
5	choose the issues that I need to raise, but ignore others. Use some upward management techniques.
4	
3	
2	
1	**Low risk**. Accept things as they are. Am very cautious about rocking the boat. Will not talk at all about my concerns for fear of retribution.
0	Cannot risk losing job and benefits.

Scale 2
Severity of problem
This second scale reflects how much negative impact your boss's behaviour has on your (and others') feelings and ability to work. The descriptions below the scale suggest what bosses do who create low, medium or high problems for their employees. Mark an *x* on the horizontal line where you believe the degree of problem severity falls.

PROBLEM SEVERITY

LOW										HIGH
0	1	2	3	4	5	6	7	8	9	10

Low severity
Most of the time, my working relationship with my boss is satisfactory. Occasionally, when very stressed, she is disorganised, un-communicative and sarcastic. It usually passes with time. Does not have serious impact.

Medium severity
Boss is tough, very demanding and critical. Hard to please. Sometimes tries to improve by reading management books and taking courses. Has made some improvement. Affects me and other employees variously depending on the situation.

High severity
Supervisor is unethical, rigid, emotionally dis-turbed, unfeeling. Impossible to do my job well because of poor information and constant criticism. Employees suffer from low morale, high turnover.

Scale 3
Risk, severity and action steps
The following scale illustrates the relationships between the level of risk you are willing to take (vertical line), the degree of severity of the boss's behaviour (horizontal line) and the most appropriate strategies (stair steps).

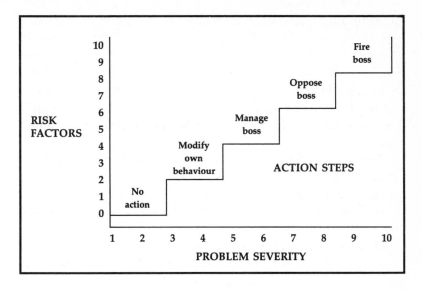

If the problem is very severe and a person is willing to take a high risk, the most successful action steps will be close to the top of the steps. You can increase your willingness to take risks by improving your work skills, getting more education or practising more assertive communication. These actions will give you more confidence and employment options and you will be less fearful of losing this job.

Real-life examples

The case studies on the following pages provide real-life examples of the relationships between employees' willingness to take risks, the supervisor's impact on employees' success and the types of steps taken in various scenarios.

Case Study 1
Good guy/bad guy

Sarah left her job at a university to work for a higher salary as a secretary for an architectural firm owned by two brothers. Fred, the owner who interviewed her, was very pleasant and appeared to be a good manager.

After working for one month, Sarah discovered that Ed, the

older brother, had daily supervisory responsibilities. He was a tyrant who yelled and swore at staff publicly and spoke demeaningly of them to other people. He hovered over Sarah's shoulder and reminded her to be careful. His continual close supervision caused her to make frequent errors.

In addition to her customary secretarial duties, both brothers had Sarah shop for family gifts and run personal errands for them.

One of the architects, Tom, was very friendly and supportive at first. Gradually, he started interrupting her work by talking to her too much. Sarah tried to handle Tom diplomatically because she valued his friendship in an otherwise unpleasant work environment.

Sarah had a good relationship with Fred, but she feared talking to him about his brother, assuming that Fred would disagree with her. So Sarah quietly accepted the situation and tried to avoid arousing Ed's anger.

Sarah was offered a new job with higher pay at the university where she used to work. To this day, Sarah omits her six months' employment with the architects from her CV.

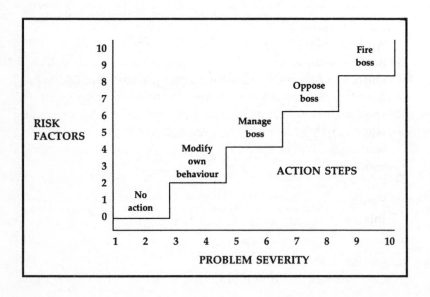

Exercise 2
Now we will assess the good guy/bad guy scenario.

1. On the risk scale from Exercise 1, where would you place
   Sarah?_____
   Why?_____

   _____

2. Where would you rate the degree of problem severity?_____
   Why?_____

   _____

3. Do you believe Sarah handled her boss–employee relationship appropriately?_____ Why or why not?_____

   _____

4. What else could Sarah have done?_____

   _____

5. What would you have done in a similar situation?_____

   _____

Author's assessment of case study 1
Sarah initially chose a low-risk approach to her relationships with Ed, Fred and Tom: doing nothing. The over-
friendly associate created more stress, particularly since
she was not assertive with him. For Sarah, the situation
was a medium- to high-risk problem severity, because she
was fearful of her boss and it increased her error rate. She
moved directly from doing nothing to firing her boss.

Sarah could have improved her situation by taking
intermediate steps:

• Clarifying her job duties through discussions with both
  owners and reopen these discussions as needed.

- Giving clear feedback to Tom that she appreciated his friendly support, but not the distractions from her work.
- Changing her thoughts and feelings about Ed's behaviour. For example, when he yelled at her publicly, she might imagine him with a funny nose and glasses. Or, she could say to herself, 'Everyone knows I'm a good secretary, and he just looks like a bad boss when he yells like this.'
- Trying to make Fred an ally. This step could be risky unless handled with great diplomacy. She could say, 'When Ed shouts at me for making mistakes, especially with other people around, it makes me so nervous that I make more errors. I'm really trying hard to get everything done properly. The other day a client came in while Ed was shouting and it was very awkward.

  'It would help me if you could suggest something I can do to improve my communications with Ed. I think it would help everyone if he didn't shout so much because it's so distracting. It must also be stressful for him. His face gets red and you can see his veins pop out.'

Case study 2
The bottleneck boss

When Bob became executive director for a social services agency, the finances were in bad shape and staff could not keep up with the requests for services. Bob moved in enthusiastically. He was committed to keeping informed and checking on the work of his 500 employees. No one could accuse Bob of laziness. He started work early and left late. When he walked down the corridor, everyone trembled, for fear he would bring them one of their mistakes with a lecture about being careful.

When a series of newspaper articles criticised Bob for his management methods and the problems that were apparently caused by employees, he asked everyone to sign a loyalty oath.

He insisted on reviewing every letter that went out to be sure it was perfect. He made it clear that no one could be trusted.

Sue, one of the departmental managers, had an increasingly difficult time with Bob's suspiciousness and checking compulsion. Paperwork got bottlenecked in Bob's office; personnel found themselves waiting indefinitely for decisions.

Sue liked her job, felt well paid, but knew she needed to take some calculated risks before her department's work slowed to a crawl. So Sue did a boss analysis. She tried to see his perspective, listed his goals and looked at his behavioural style. Then, she assessed how serious the problem was and decided she could manage a medium–high risk. However, she wanted to start at the lowest risk level that would bring positive results.

The following scale reflects Sue's decisions:

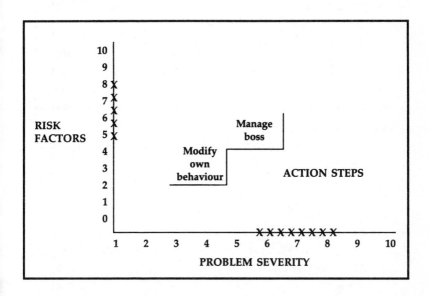

It was apparent to Sue that Bob was a perfectionist and his style became exaggerated under stress. Bob felt stressed by the newspaper articles, so he was suspicious and distrustful.

Sue laid out and followed several strategies over a six-month period:

- Provided lots of written and oral information.
- Asked his opinion on the best way to speed up the process; explain the consequences of delayed paperwork.
- Whenever possible, gave him positive feedback about the improvements in the agency's finances and accuracy of record keeping.
- Demonstrated loyalty to him by making him look good in public.
- Avoided a power push.

Exercise 3
Now assess the bottleneck boss.

1. What do you believe will be the likely outcome of Sue's efforts?_____
2. If she is unsuccessful, what else could she do?_____
   _____
3. What would you do if you worked for a boss like this?_____
   _____

Author's assessment of case 2
Sue's thoughtful approach is likely to be successful if she has the luxury of waiting for Bob to move faster while the rest of the agency slows down and waits for him. She might suggest that her peers and employees follow the same strategy. Together, they increase the potential for improvement if they keep Bob's paranoia under control and get him to delegate more responsibility. If Bob continues to engage in his bottleneck actions, Sue might need to escalate her risk quotient with more direct and possibly confrontational steps. Working in an agency under public censure could affect her future career. Sue might set a mental deadline to find another job if the situation worsens.

CHAPTER 10
Snakes or Ladders

Most people are interested in climbing the career ladder and prefer not to slip down the 'snake' to an untimely and involuntary employment exit. Employees who feel most successful have learned how to achieve their own goals (security, recognition, autonomy) while contributing to the company's success.

Assess yourself

Both you and your supervisor are responsible for assessing how your performance contributes to your mutual success. The following self-assessment score sheet will pinpoint areas for improvement and help you to decide whether you will stagnate or surge ahead in your career.

Many of the strategies will help to protect your career from the ravages of a dreadful supervisor. For example, by building skills, reputation and support networks, you will have more flexibility to take risks.

Exercise 1. Your career advancement score sheet
Rate the frequency with which you perform the following activities listed overleaf. Use the scale: 5 = always; 4 = most of the time; 3 = sometimes; 2 = rarely; 1 = never.

Score
_____

1. Attend work-related conferences when available   _____
2. Advise decision makers of my interest in advancement, according to the procedures and customs of the organisation   _____
3. Participate in meetings or other group activities   _____
4. Receive positive feedback from others without asking for it   _____
5. Speak positively about my company to outside people   _____
6. Keep informed of requirements for career advancement in my company and field   _____
7. Read items in my speciality to keep up to date   _____
8. Read outside my field to learn new skills   _____
9. Attend seminars, courses, speeches to expand skills   _____
10. Observe the unwritten rules of my organisation such as dress code, behavioural style and friendship patterns   _____
11. Seek increased responsibilities such as serving on committees, project teams, etc   _____
12. Belong to at least one work-related organisation such as a trade association   _____
13. Serve on a committee of at least one community or professional organisation   _____
14. Talk to friends and relatives about my career plans   _____
15. Expand my circle of acquaintances to include people who can help me with career advancement   _____
16. Complete assignments on time   _____
17. Go the extra mile to satisfy customers   _____
18. Receive above average to excellent evaluations   _____
19. Adhere to the policies and procedures of the company   _____
20. Make changes or suggest ways to improve work   _____
21. Perform work well   _____
22. Maintain exemplary attendance records   _____
23. Communicate clearly   _____
24. Seek comment on the quality of my work   _____

Score

---

25. Work on aspects of my performance that need improvement ____
26. Develop and implement personal career plans based on an annual self-assessment ____
27. Be known as a self-starter ____
28. Display a positive attitude ____
29. Get along well with peers, supervisors, clients and ____ others
30. If I have a personal conflict, find ways to resolve it ____

Add up your responses and compare your score with the table below.

Very low	1–30
Low	31–60
Medium	61–90
High	91–120
Very high	121 and above

Very low scores indicate you are not moving ahead. You may believe many of the career myths including the one that people get ahead by just doing their work and minding their own business. Perhaps you feel you do not have enough time for the 'extras' such as reading.

Low scores suggest that you have developed career skills in some areas but not in others. Identify where you need to improve. Is shyness holding you back from promoting yourself?

Medium scores imply that you are not over-fearful of reaching for success. Sharpen your career goals and continue to use self-promotion techniques.

High scores indicate self-confidence and ambition. You have an excellent prognosis for success. You know what your goal is and how to reach it.

Very high scores suggest that you are probably already reaping career success. You need to guard against over-confidence and brashness so you do not offend others. Keep your performance quality high and be considerate of people around you.

Evaluating your scoresheet

Quality work is essential, but it is not the sole prerequisite for career success. The right people must be aware of your work and how you contribute to the organisation.

High visibility can be a double-edged sword, however, advertising both strengths and weaknesses. A good barometer of your image is whether or not you receive unsolicited compliments and recognition, particularly from superiors.

If you need to raise your positive image, explore techniques that feel natural. Contribute a new idea or solution to a problem; offer assistance or say thank you to others.

To expand your flexibility and options, commit yourself to a life-long programme of education. Today's workplace is in the midst of an information revolution. The pressure to update your knowledge and skills comes from all sides: the impact of computers, a constant influx of well-trained employees and the increasing number of job seekers. Read, take classes and observe your colleagues. Expand your horizons into related or new fields.

Observe the unwritten rules of your firm. Do not violate your company's codes unless you want negative publicity. For example, pay attention to the dress code, interpersonal forms of address and subtle requirements for overtime. A warning light should flash in your mind if your value system conflicts with your company's customs and philosophy.

Successful employment is a contact game. You need personal associations within and outside your workplace. A supportive circle of associates and friends provides information.

But all the visibility and contacts in the world will be purpose-less unless the quality of your work is satisfactory. Find out what your job requires. Develop your skills, then make the extra effort to achieve excellence.

Exercise 2. Your self-improvement action plan
Your scores on the career advancement score sheet may suggest areas of your career that need more attention. The score sheet is divided into five groups: *visibility* (questions 1–5), *education* (questions 6–10), *contacts* (questions 11–15), *work quality* (questions 16–25), and *personal* (questions 26–30).

Review the statements in each of the five groups to develop your own action plan. Examples are provided as thought starters.

A. **Visibility (1–5)**
   Example: 'I will attend the next annual meeting of the Society of Internal Auditors.'
   Insert your action plan to improve *visibility*.

B. **Education (6–11)**
   Example: 'I will subscribe to *Harvard Business Review* and read articles on finance.'
   Insert your action plan to improve *education*.

C. **Contacts (11–15)**
   Example: 'Next week, I will ask Bill to add me to the commu-nications task force.'
   Insert your action plan to improve *contacts*.

D. **Work quality (16–25)**
   Example: 'The idea I have to reduce paperwork needs to be tested. I'll discuss it with Betty at our next supervisory meeting.'
   Insert your action plan to improve *work quality*.

E. **Personal (26–30)**

Example: 'I will let Ed know that his frequent interruptions are making it very hard for me to get his work done on time.'

Insert your action plan to improve *personal*.

How to achieve good performance evaluations

For most people the performance evaluation process is extremely painful. It has traditionally been used as a time to report bad news to the individual, such as all the mistakes made during the past year. Not only is it personally painful to hear criticism, but the evaluation process is often tied to salary adjustments for the coming year.

More enlightened organisations and their managers are learning how to give feedback regularly and to use the periodic, formal evaluation as an opportunity to summarise feedback already provided as well as to set annual goals.

Whether or not your organisation does this, you can take several steps to ensure that your performance evaluation is fair, accurate and positive.

Step 1
Set performance goals
Before anyone can measure anything, there must be a standard against which it can be compared. Prioritise your goals and discuss them with your boss. You may wish to include personal goals such as gaining a degree or developing a new skill. Quantify your goals and always have someone else proofread them.

Depending upon your level of communication with your manager, you may choose to share your personal goals. Obviously, if you are interested in a promotion, your boss may be able to clarify what it requires.

Exercise 3. Goals work sheet
Modify the following work sheet format to meet your needs:

My organisational goals for (dates)   **to**   **are:**

Goals	Measurable results
1. _____	_____
2. _____	_____
3. _____	_____

My personal goals for (dates)   **to**   **are:**

Goals	Measurable results
1. _____	_____
2. _____	_____
3. _____	_____

Step 2
Keep score all year long
Bosses like to be kept informed about your progress towards your goals. By keeping records of achievements and problems, you can keep your supervisor informed, keep yourself on track and have documentation to support the formal performance evaluation.

Exercise 4. Achievement record
Records provide specific information that is directly related to the agreed organisational goals. Modify the following work sheet as needed:

Goal	Evidence of achievement	Evidence of problems
1.	_____	_____
2.	_____	_____
3.	_____	_____
4.	_____	_____

Step 3
Become a partner in your performance evaluation
You can prepare for the formal performance evaluation. Ask

your boss for a meeting. Express your desire to be a productive employee. Say you want to discuss company expectations and your goals. Offer to show your boss your achievement records. Ask for specifics.

Handling criticism

Many employees find it more difficult to accept criticism than compliments from their boss. But the truly successful professional needs to know how to improve.

Exercise 5. How do I handle criticism?

1. Place a 'plus' (+) by those situations you feel you handle appropriately; a 'minus' (−) by those situations you avoid handling; and a 'zero' (0) by those you may handle, but they cause internal stress or anxiety.

_____ In a department meeting you make an important statement that everyone ignores.

_____ Your boss criticises your job performance.

_____ Your boss makes a negative remark about your new haircut.

_____ You hear from a colleague that your boss is upset about a comment you made in yesterday's staff meeting.

_____ Your boss criticises you unjustifiably.

_____ At lunch, a manager makes a negative comment about a project you are in charge of.

_____ You are depressed and your boss criticises you for your bad attitude.

_____ A manager from another department sends you a memo criticising your latest idea.

_____ You complete an assignment to the best of your ability and are told that you could have done a better job.

_____ You ask your boss to consider you for leadership responsibilities on an exciting new project and are turned down.

2. In the situations that you marked with a plus, list the actions you take that cause you to be effective:

_____

_____

_____

3. Analyse those situations you marked with a minus and a zero. Write down why those situations are difficult for you to handle and the actions you typically take:

A. Why difficult?   **B. Typical response**

_____   _____

_____   _____

_____   _____

_____   _____

Types of criticism
The three types of criticism that you might experience are unjustified criticism, criticism that is vague or a difference of opinion, and valid criticism.

- **Unjustified criticism** may come as a result of not living up to the fantasy our boss has created for us. Often, bosses do not tell us their expectations. For criticism to be helpful, we must ask for specific, concrete objectives so we can understand our boss's expectations and take action if we choose.

- **Vague criticism** may indicate a difference of opinion. Your boss may think other values and methods of doing something are better than yours.

- **Valid criticism** is the most difficult type of criticism for us to handle because we have to admit we are wrong. We tend to give more significance to our mistake than necessary, to make it more important than it is. We must recognise that we all make mistakes. The more active and fruitful our lives, the more we will receive criticism.

Coping with criticism from our boss

Once the criticism is made, the receiver has control of the next step. It is up to us to decide whether we believe the criticism has merit and is worth acting upon.

There are basically three stages you go through when handling criticism: *awareness*, *assessment* and *action*.

In the awareness stage, your natural instincts take over. You usually respond by counter-attacking defensively or accepting the criticism silently at face value.

In the assessment stage you consider how the criticism was delivered, the intention of your boss, and how valid you believe the criticism to be. In the final stage, you decide on any action you want to take in response to the criticism.

If you can be assertive when being criticised, you will remain confident and cool during the process. An assertive approach strives to maintain a win–win attitude in which you allow your boss to have an opinion while maintaining your self-esteem.

Responding to unjustified criticism

The first thing you must do when your supervisor criticises you unjustifiably is to put up a psychological barrier so that you do not take the criticism personally. One of the basic foundations for handling criticism effectively is self-confidence.

You must be good at what you do and believe in yourself or you will probably crumble under your boss's criticism. If you believe in yourself, your abilities, skills and knowledge, criticism is much less threatening, and you will be able to take it less personally. You must choose to let the criticism have no impact. Do not counter-criticise or counter-manipulate or, worse still, talk behind your manager's back.

Fogging

When faced with unjustified criticism, 'fog' the situation. Fogging is acknowledging the possibility that the criticism may contain some truth. Say, for example: 'You could be right about . . .', 'You might be right about . . .', 'Perhaps I could . . .', 'Maybe I should . . .', 'What you say makes some sense . . .' or 'I'll consider your input . . .'.

If your boss criticises how you handled a customer, say, 'Perhaps I could have been more effective.' Then ask for specifics on what to do differently. This way you merely acknowledge that perhaps you could have been more effective (we can always improve), which satisfies the critic.

Request specific feedback
This example incorporates a second technique, requesting specific feedback, which is very effective with vague criticism. This technique uses questions to focus on the future instead of dwelling on the error. It moves you directly into the action stage. You can use the following list of responses to get specific feedback.

- 'What specifically did I do that . . .?'
- 'If you were in my shoes, what would you do differently?'
- 'I'm not sure I understand what you mean. Can you please give me some examples of where I have done that?'
- 'Is that all you can think of that I could do to improve my performance?'

A companion technique to requesting specific feedback is called the *echo* technique. It will help you to listen more effectively and gain information from your boss that you can use to rectify the problem. You simply repeat the last three to six words of your critic.

Case scenario
Boss: 'I'm not pleased with how this report looks. Please take another crack at it.'
You: 'What specifically do you not like about the report?'
Boss: 'I don't like the format of the report.'
You: 'The format of the report?'
Boss: 'Yes, the format. It seems a bit jumbled in places.'

You: 'A bit jumbled in places?'

Boss: 'Yes . . . particularly on the third page.'

You: 'The third page?'

Boss: 'Well, if you would rearrange the statistics with the text on page three, I think it would be easier to read.'

You: 'So, if I rearrange the statistics with the text on page three, the report would look better?'

Boss: 'Yes.'

You: 'Is there anything else I should do differently with this report to make it more readable?'

Admit the truth

The last technique is the simplest and most effective when coping with valid criticism: admit the truth. You made a mistake, so admit it rather than making excuses, apologising profusely or overcompensating for your error.

Sample responses

'You're right. I didn't make my sales quota this month and this is what I'm planning to do to meet the quota next month . . .'

'That's right. I didn't use the correct formula when I was analysing the numbers. I'll rework the report using the correct figures, now that I know them. Thanks for pointing that out.'

'You're right. I probably could have thought that through more carefully. What would you have done?'

Valid criticism scenario

Boss: 'I think you could've handled the staff meeting more effectively this morning.'

You: 'I wasn't happy with how things went either. Next time I'm planning to send out an agenda in advance so we can all be better prepared and use the time effectively. Do you have any other ideas on how I could make the meeting more effective?'

Exercise 6. Putting your skills to the test

Now practise your skills in handling criticism. Use a combination of the fogging, requesting specific feedback/echo and admit the truth techniques. Write your answers on the lines provided.

1. Things haven't been going well for you lately, you are feeling a bit low. Your boss says to you, 'What's been bugging you lately . . . you have a very negative attitude.'

   _____

   _____

   _____

   _____

2. You have just completed an assignment. Your boss looks over it and comments, 'I really had expected more from you as a senior professional in our group,.'

   _____

   _____

   _____

   _____

3. You hear from a colleague that your boss is upset about a comment you made in yesterday's staff meeting. You would like to 'clear the air' with your boss.

   _____

   _____

   _____

   _____

Potential responses to situations 1–3 (from page 103)
1. 'Perhaps I have been a bit low lately (fogging). Has this caused a problem in my performance that I have been unaware of?' (request specific comment)
2. 'What specifically had you expected from me as a senior professional in this group?' or 'What would you have done differently?' (requesting specific comment)
3. 'I sense you were upset about the staff meeting yesterday. Was there anything that I said or did that is bothering you?' (request specific comment)

CHAPTER 11
The Final Episode

You have now completed the book and you should be closer to an effective working partnership. It is your right and responsibility to manage your manager. It is part of your job.

You have the most vested interest in your career, personal satisfaction and happiness. These ideas will help you to understand and focus on the big picture, communicate for greater impact and build bridges with your boss. You now know how to confront your supervisor with compassion and have analysed your boss's behavioural style. You have learned how to manage those time-management monsters and how to build your career ladder. The rest is up to you.

You really have three choices when it comes to your relationship with your manager:

1. Change your manager
2. Change your environment
3. Change yourself.

Of these three choices, you have control over yourself only. So what action are you going to take as a result of reading this book?

If you have already changed the way you cope with your boss, you may have experienced some of these benefits:

- Reduced physical and mental stress
- Increased opportunity for recognition and promotion
- The company implemented my ideas
- Increase in my self-confidence, motivation and morale

- Increased respect from colleagues
- Helped me to make a career decision about whether to leave the job
- Anticipated and avoided problems with my boss
- Improved the quality and quantity of work
- Increased enjoyment of my job.

If you do not take action, not much will change.

We hope this book has helped you to accept the things you cannot change in your job, has given you the courage to change the things you can, and that you have gained some knowledge in understanding the difference between the two.

Further Reading from Kogan Page

Delegating for Results, Robert B Maddux
Effective Meeting Skills: How to Make Meetings More Productive, Marion E Haynes
Effective Performance Appraisals, Robert B Maddux*
Effective Presentation Skills, Steve Mandel
The Fifty-Minute Supervisor: A Guide for the Newly Promoted, Elwood N Chapman
How to Communicate Effectively, Bert Decker*
How to Develop a Positive Attitude, Elwood N Chapman*
How to Develop Assertiveness, Sam R Lloyd
How to Motivate People, Twyla Dell*
Learning to Lead, Pat Heim and Elwood N Chapman
Make Every Minute Count: How to Manage Your Time Effectively, Marion E Haynes*
Managing Disagreement Constructively, Herbert S Kindler
Managing Organisational Change, C Scott and D T Jaffe
Managing Quality Customer Service, William B Martin
Office Management, Marilyn Manning and Patricia Haddock
Project Management, Marion E Haynes
Risk Taking, Herbert S Kindler
Successful Negotiation, Robert B Maddux
Team Building: An Exercise in Leadership, Robert B Maddux

*Also available on cassette.